DECISIO

DECISION TAKING

by Colin Chase

The Industrial Society

First published 1976 by
The Industrial Society
Peter Runge House
3 Carlton House Terrace
London SW1Y 5DG
Telephone: 01–839 4300

Fifth edition 1989
© *The Industrial Society, 1976, 1979, 1980, 1983, 1989*

ISBN 0 85290 441 X

British Library Cataloguing in Publication Data

Sargent, Andrew
    Decision taking.—5th ed
    1. Management. Decision making
    I. Title   II. Chase, Colin   III. Series
    658.4'03

Typeset by Ace Filmsetting Ltd, Frome, Somerset
Printed and bound in Great Britain by Belmont Press, Northampton

CONTENTS

FOREWORD

Whatever the discipline or level of management, the responsibilities of a manager are many and various. It is their job to produce results with essentially just two resources—people and time.

To maximise the potential of both, most managers need some reminders and basic guidelines to help them.

The Notes for Managers series provides succinct yet comprehensive coverage of key management issues and skills. The short time it takes to read each title will pay dividends in terms of utilising one of those key resources—people.

This book serves as a summary of the experience of *managing* participation. It recognises our fundamental reality that, whether managers like it or not, the employees are the people who ultimately decide whether commitment and co-operation are to be given in the implementation of decisions affecting them. Managers can decide what they want about what needs to be done, but making it happen is an entirely different matter.

ALISTAIR GRAHAM
Director, The Industrial Society

I

DECISION TAKING

1

SETTING THE SCENE

We face an ever increasing rate of change, both with the society in which we live, and at the work place.

The development time of most products must now be measured in months, rather than years, to remain competitive within the international market-place. Services are under constant pressure for improvement, whether by local authorities, health service, hotel and leisure industry or travel. People demand more, the knowledge of availability is greater, and the scope for choice is continually increasing as previous market barriers and regulatory systems disappear.

The challenge to those who manage is to decide how best to cope with these changes; how to react to external pressures on the company; how to avoid being *always* in the situation of reacting, and instead be in the position of taking the lead by being a master of change. Most of these decisions regarding new courses of action will take us into areas where clear answers seldom exist. This will demand our assessment and judgement about people and activities now and in the future. Frequently this will involve compromising priorities, making choices, evaluating ideas and deciding against conflicting criteria. In essence, this is what management is mainly about—taking decisions and getting them implemented.

Possibly, it is getting them implemented that causes the greatest problem. This may be through insufficient thought being given to the factors affecting how the decision is translated into action. Alternatively, that the worst fears are confirmed as the results of the decision take effect and people react to these results.

Clearly, anyone in a position of authority carrying a title of 'manager', 'supervisor', 'officer', 'executive', 'chargehand', 'captain' or any other that equates to demands of leadership, must take all possible steps to be as professional as possible in the field of decision taking. Our very future depends upon the decisions all sorts of people take every day at work. Decisions affect how others operate, what work is done, whether they even eventually have a job or, indeed, their health and safety.

We need, therefore, to address the issues of decision taking from a people aspect. From the aspect of establishing the manager as a leader who is capable of planning the future, rather than reacting piecemeal to each new event that impinges on the organisation. This is the area of decision taking that will be addressed in this book: considering how we can best approach the decision taking process in a manner that will improve the quality of our decisions and, subsequently, the manner in which they are implemented.

2

THE DECISION TAKER
AS A LEADER

Coupled with the increasing rate of change is the increasingly high level of expectation of people at work. As products and services change, better entertainment systems become available, extended travel a feature of vacations, car ownership an accepted norm, education and training a continuing feature of life, so will the demand of managers to manage by ability and not by status become more pressing. This results in a much more open style, where steps are taken to keep people informed; to ensure that they understand the aims of the organisation and their own individual roles within it. Somehow, the environment has to be created which encourages people to make use of their skills and ingenuity to the common value of the organisation. This leads to establishing forums for joint discussions, generating ideas and suggestions as well as questioning current activities.

Through involving people in the decision process, there grows a fear that management loses the initiative. What we need to understand is that the process of decision taking involves people in a manner which contributes to the effectiveness of the decision and its implementation *without* undermining the vital leadership role of an individual leader.

What, therefore, we must develop is the ability to combine the many skills that encapsulate the manager as a leader, in being an effective decision taker.

3

STAGES OF
DECISION TAKING

The art of leadership is in making difficult things simple. In a similar way, a checklist for decision taking should be developed that enables ease of reference for most effective use. From the gathered wisdom of many managers and leaders our decision taking process can be based on five principle stages.

The five C's of decision taking and implementation

1 *Consider.* The thinking starts now! Define the objective; consider the problem.
2 *Consult.* The stage at which you take initiatives to involve those affected.
3 *Commit.* Ensuring that appropriate action will be taken.
4 *Communicate.* The stage at which you explain what has been decided and why.
5 *Check.* The need for visible leadership in ensuring the decision actually works.

This is our foundation (*see* Table 1) on which we can build more detailed actions. First, though, it is necessary to make three major points about these stages.

● It cannot always be a progressive step-by-step process. Sometimes it is necessary to go back a stage and repeat part of the loop. For example, following consultation with others and establishing further facts, it becomes clear that we need to return to the initial question or problem and reconsider the objective. However, we must be careful that this is not an eternal loop for ducking decisions! This will be taken up later in the next chapter.

- Consultation is not applicable in all situations. Through reasons of policy, time, or the extent of an emergency, the manager may well be in the situation of moving straight from the 'consider' stage to the 'commit'. This is all part of the vital thought process that must happen at the outset, so that the implications of omitting the consultation are understood, and appropriate actions taken to cope with this when at the 'communicate' stage.

- There is no recognition of negotiation in this 5-stage process of decision taking. This is because negotiation is a separate stage when no one leader has the authority to take the decision. When that authority does exist, we must ensure that neither 'consult' nor 'communicate' degenerate into negotiation. It is vital that we either have one person taking the decision and being accountable, or a joint party negotiating. In either event, consultation before meeting at the negotiation table is important, as are the communication processes that would follow. During negotiation, however, we have more than one organisation system conducting these two stages (e.g. management seeking views and explaining outcome, whilst union officials or employee representatives would be doing likewise).

Table 1. Decision taking—key actions

Consider	Consult	Commit	Communicate	Check
Ultimate objective	Others likely to be affected	A plan of action within time scale	Face-to-face in teams	Decision is being implemented Walk the job
ESTABLISH Problems Cause and effect Who is affected Time scales Constraints	ENCOURAGE Attendance Suggestions Listening Creativity Time to think	Take the decision Write it down Be committed and enthusiastic	EXPLAIN Sell the decision Check understanding	EVALUATE Understanding and acceptance Training Standards Quality Delegation Rewards Is it achieving the objective?
What, Why, When, Who, Where, How.				

7

4

KEY ACTIONS FOR
DECISION TAKING

Regardless of the complexity of the decision it is vital to be clear at the outset who will ultimately take that decision. Managers are more enthusiastic about carrying out decisions that they have made themselves. Doubtless most of us know examples of marginal, or difficult decisions that have been turned into highly effective ones as a result of the commitment and enthusiasm of the person who took it. One lesson to be learned from this is that it is much more practical to delegate decision taking as far down the line as possible.

This is much easier said than done, since doing so involves trusting people and carrying the can for subordinates who make mistakes, as they inevitably will, from time to time. A decision-taking policy shows that there are enormous rewards to be gained from trusting people, and taking the risk, rather than *not* trusting them, with all the accompanying problems of time, failing initiative and morale, and enjoying the false luxury of being indispensible.

The actions that follow, under the five stages we have already identified, are as applicable to a senior manager taking policy decisions, as they are to the supervisor tackling today's problems. The major difference relates to the timescales involved in taking the decision, and in the extent of future impact. For those involved, however, the distinction is of scant interest—either the decision will be effective or it will not.

It is incumbent on leaders at every level to think carefully about the following actions and to be continually looking for ways to be 'in charge of their own destiny'.

1 **Consider**

The decision-taking process starts when it is apparent that some management action or initiative is necessary. The first action is to give yourself time to think. Consider if the real problem is being tackled and not merely the superficial symptoms of an underlying factor, or, indeed, whether intervention is actually necessary. Some problems solve themselves without the need for outside help. In some circumstances, the best possible decision to take *is to take no decision.* Next, however, you should consider what your aim is; what is it that you want to achieve? Finally it is sensible to establish what are the constraints within which action must be taken.

Establish

- What information do I need? How do I get it?
- Is the decision mine? Am I assuming too much authority? Am I undermining someone else's responsibilities?
- Who is likely to be affected by the decision?
- What other constraints are there likely to be? (E.g. policies, precedent, legal, financial, external influences.)
- Time-scales. What is the *latest* possible date or time by which the decision must be taken? If we decide too soon, we may deprive ourselves of information or relevant factors which have not yet come to light. If we delay, we may prevent others in the organisation from getting on with their jobs, thus wasting resources.

Finally, ask yourself: 'What would happen if no decision were taken at all?' (In this way, you may well save yourself a great deal of time and trouble.)

Checklist

- Has the *real* problem been defined?
- What is the decision intended to achieve?
- By when must the decision be taken?
- What other constraints are there?

- What would be the effect if no decision were taken?
- What information is needed?
- Should it be delegated?

2 Consult

Experience shows that group decision taking is not usually practical. Yet at the same time, all the evidence is that, when people are not involved in decisions that affect them, their commitment is difficult to obtain. The most effective way of involving people is to adopt the approach of *consultation before decision.* But the crucial word is *'before'.* Consulting people *after* decisions have been made is rarely productive and frequently leads to resentment, as many managers have found to their cost.

In cases where consultation is not appropriate, it is vital to plan the communication stage well, and to make every effort to achieve acceptance of the decision. Where consultation processes have taken place, there is far greater understanding of the intentions of management, often creating an atmosphere of wishing to help on the part of the workforce.

It cannot be emphasised too often that managers have to get results through people. Others must carry out their decisions. Managers therefore need co-operation and commitment. To get these, they must convey to an increasingly better educated, articulate, and critical workforce, the facts of the situation relating to the decision.

But people perceive facts and situations from different standpoints. They see things differently; their feelings are involved; their interests are affected; their jobs and security may appear to be threatened and, above all, they often have the knowledge and experience which springs from having to carry out decisions and do the actual work. They therefore have much to contribute to the decision making process, but must clearly understand that the decision itself is the responsibility of the appointed leader.

Encourage consultation

Consultation can, in many instances, be limited to the immediate work group, as is often the case with operational decisions. But some tactical and strategic decisions affect far wider areas of an organisation, and this calls for the use of whatever formal consultation arrangement exists. The organisation may or may not be unionised, but, where unions are recognised, they must be included. A meeting should, therefore, be called with those involved, or their representatives, and the maximum amount of information made available.

Increasingly, decisions cut across conventional organisation boundaries. Lateral teamwork is becoming more important, and, frequently, it is of value to establish a multi-disciplinary team for specific problem solving activities. However, it is vital that *vertical* teamwork is strengthened *before* forming teams for generating ideas and suggestions that cut across the functional structure.

Working to timescales

The timing of consultation will often call for sensitivity and good judgement. There is a strong case for consulting as early as is practicable, so as to allow as much time as possible to weigh up the pro's and con's of the situation. But, on the other hand, the desirability of early consultation has also to be weighed against the need to avoid long, drawn out, and possibly destructive discussions of contentious issues, as well as raising hopes or apprehensions unnecessarily early. In any event, it is wise to set a time limit so that everyone knows when consultation will stop and a decision be taken.

Checklist

- Have all the people who should be consulted been identified?
- Has the information which should be tabled, including the constraints, been assembled?
- Have meetings been convened of consultative committees and trade union representatives?

- Has the timing of consultation been chosen with care and a date been set for concluding the process?
- Have you attempted to think *outside* the problem by creating a task force and using creative techniques such as brainstorming?
- Are you fully prepared to listen to ideas and suggestions, without jumping to conclusions?

3   Commit

Having completed the first two stages, all that remains is to *take the decision.* One must weigh up the gathered views and opinions, evaluate the ideas and suggestions put forward, and review the facts. The result is a rational consideration of the risks, probabilities, and rewards.

In actuality, many managers are given an uncomfortable time by this process. Why is this so? Many reasons could be given, but the chances are that the answer is reflected in one, or more, of the following:

- insufficient time to think at stage 1; being under pressure, or simply failing to resist your own burning desire to get on and act
- failing to listen at stage 2; either not consulting at all, or doing it in such a way that you were not really receptive to the views, opinions and suggestions of others
- failing to assemble sufficient relevant data at stage 2; or assembling so much that the important issues were submerged under superfluities
- failing to face the issues within the timescale set for action, and not progressing beyond stage 2.

Far better instead to:

- review the information already assembled—which should include feelings as well as facts
- try to assess the extent to which the absence of some information will affect the quality of the decision

- list the operations and the arguments for and against
- give yourself time to think; if possible, sleep on it
- discipline yourself to decide within the set timescale.

Making up your mind

The decision, when arrived at, can sometimes be appropriately described as 'the least worst' decision rather than 'the best' decision since there are bound to be some disadvantages and some interests adversely affected. For this reason, decisions sometimes demand courage and resolution to face up to unpopularity and dissent. Once the decision has been taken, be committed and enthusiastic about the plan of action, however finely balanced the decision.

Checklist

- Review the objectives established at Stage 1.
- Classify them according to importance—what *must* we achieve? What would we like to achieve?
- List all options (and feelings).
- Evaluate options against objectives.
- Choose the best option and assess the consequences— if these are too great the second best option may have to be considered.
- Make a serious attempt to see the consequences of each option.
- Take the decisions—it may be the 'least worst'.
- Record the decision and the plan in writing.
- Be committed and enthusiastic.

Group decisions

Because decisions frequently affect an entire group of people, some managers are tempted to implement decisions because they will be popularly received by the group—but not necessarily because they are the right course of action!

However tempting, it is worth remembering that:

- group decisions are frequently an outward and visible sign of consensus or compromise, for which few people feel any real enthusiasm—UNLESS THE DECISION IS OBVIOUS
- they frequently result from majorities outvoting minorities, but make no provision for the needs of the latter
- nobody remains accountable for what happens—if queries or problems arise, people feel free to pass the buck.

It is seldom worthwhile passing the decision taking process to a group. Teamwork is more likely to be weakened by providing the team with total responsibility.

4 Communicate

More decisions flounder because of poor communications than for any other single reason. Most managers all too frequently have experience of this, and it is appropriate to review the key points.

First, it is vital to secure peoples' commitment to decisions by communicating face-to-face. It is a selling operation, explaining the decision so that people have the opportunity to ask questions. This way, we all find it easier to understand and accept—even though we may not agree. If we only use the notice board, company newspaper, scan light, or a video, the decision is likely to fail. Any of these communication methods are invaluable back-up tools to the team meeting or equivalent forum, according to the nature and impact of the decision.

Second, it must be remembered that it is the job of whoever takes the decision to ensure that it gets communicated. Part of the problem at stage 3 may be hesitancy in taking the decision because of concern at facing the consequences of that decision. Managers who are leaders do not evade the importance of communicating face-to-face and ensuring that the decision is communicated down and across all necessary management lines.

Team briefing

Many of the problems of communication can be overcome by installing team briefing to ensure that the decision and the reasons for it are transmitted right the way down the line, from the level at which it is taken, to those whom it actually affects. It also ensures that the message is put over only by those who can be accountable for doing so. In this way, managers can check that even an unpopular decision is enthusiastically and properly put over—and it is enthusiasm that forms the springboard for a decision's success.

You can still insist that subordinates who manage others *put a message across* and do not fall back on weak apologies such as: 'It's not my fault, it was management's decision'. Team briefing is a good way of making sure that managers do actually *manage*, and that they are reinforced and consolidated in their rightful position as leaders of the work group (*see Team briefing* and *The manager's responsibility for communication*, in this series).

Explain

The crucial points to communicate are the decisions and the reason for them, *plus* examples that will make the message real for the receiver. People need to understand when the decision will be implemented, who will be affected and how and, finally, what the procedure is for registering a complaint or grievance.

It is the added dimension of 'explanation' to information which helps reduce people's fear of change, and also effectively combats the grapevine, that rumour network frequently giving remarkably accurate information, completely distorted reasons, and, as a result, severe management headaches!

Checklist

- Have the methods of implementing a decision been planned?
- Have all those affected been briefed in teams, with facts and reasons, face-to-face?
- Are the channels for feedback fully understood?
- Have all those affected accepted the decision?

5 Check

Finally, there is a need to know whether the decision you have taken is actually working. Naturally, a great deal of information can be obtained through the normal channels of returns and statistics, not to mention the feedback from trade union representatives and from briefing groups. But there is no substitute for going out to see for yourself as well.

By going out and walking the job, managers can observe the operation for which they are responsible by talking with people. They can gauge a great deal, not just from what people actually say, but also from the way that they say it. They can develop their ability to observe the signs of effective team work, and can often catch the first 'wisp of smoke' from an impending crisis. Also, observing for themselves enables them to determine whether or not any corrective action is necessary. Above all, however, it enables people to see that managers are acknowledging their own responsibility!

If the decision is working then we need to know that, so as to identify good practices and promote a positive climate of motivation by 'catching people doing things right'. If the decision is not working, then we need to review potential weak areas:

● inadequate information
● poor judgement
● lack of courage
● inadequate plans for implementation
● a breakdown in briefing
● lack of enthusiasm on the part of management.

Evaluate
● whether people have understood the briefing and accepted the implications
● whether anyone needs training as a result of what is now being actioned
● that standards are being achieved

- whether quality can be improved
- whether authority can now be delegated for subsequent decisions
- whether any rewards are justified
- is corrective action needed?

Nowadays, we must take decisions by drawing upon other people's skills and experiences whilst still having the leadership responsibilities of deciding which course of action. Equally, we must have the commitment to see that course of action implemented, with all that is required in standards of quality of goods and services. Decision taking draws upon all our skills of communicating. It also demands making the time to think and getting others to think, whilst keeping to your timescales and not ducking issues. There is much to commend the stages and key actions contained in this booklet. One may even become a better leader in the process.

APPENDIX

COMPANY POLICIES—DECISION TAKING

A number of organisations have evolved policies on decision taking. These, of course, amount to little more than guidelines—how *can* you legislate for every situation? However, at the same time, they can be enormously helpful once the right sort of environment has been created. They help managers sort out the priorities and make them more consistent people to work for or deal with. Here are two typical policies, written down, after consultation, by chief executives.

Policy 1

- Decisions should be delegated as far down the management chain as practicable.

- Sufficient preparatory work, often by specialists, should be carried out to ensure that a meaningful discussion with employees or their representatives can take place.

- Managers should take the final decision only after considering fairly and fully the facts and the opinions of employees or their representatives.

- Employees or their representatives should be involved as early as possible before any decision is taken on changes which may affect their conditions of employment, their work or their working environment.

- All relevant information should be provided in terms which can be readily understood.

- Many day-to-day decisions can be made without direct employee involvement on every occasion if general parameters are already established.

Policy 2

Delegation. Our policy on decision taking is based upon the principle that the most highly motivated decisions are those that we take ourselves. Therefore, wherever possible, decisions in this organisation should be delegated to whoever has to carry out the action.

Consultation. Where a decision is to be taken that affects either an individual or a number of people, it is the job of the leader of that group to take the decision *after* consulting. Leaders should therefore, first, sincerely seek people's views, except on those few occasions when time prevents. *They will also consult employee representatives, where appropriate.* Having done this, they will then take the decision themselves, basing it upon what they believe to be right, but having taken into account the views expressed, their own experience, and judgement.

Explanation. Deciders will explain *why* they have taken the decision, in order to help people to live with it and enthusiastically carry it out, *even it they don't agree.*

Consistency. Where a decision has been taken at a higher level, and affects people, it is the responsibility of the leaders at *every* level to see that it is implemented energetically, *whether they agree or not.*

Company objectives. When taking decisions, the guiding principle will be the greatest possible achievement of the organisation's objectives. The decision taker will try to be as positive and consistent as possible. If events show that the decision is wrong, the deciders must be prepared to admit that they made a mistake and change the decision accordingly.

Right of appeal. If somebody believes that the decision involves an injustice and not merely a difference of opinion, they must be encouraged to make use of the grievance procedure or, after talking to their immediate boss, go and see the level above